An Apology for Printers

AN
APOLOGY FOR
PRINTERS

Benjamin Franklin

Edited and with an introduction by
Randolph Goodman; *a prefatory
note by* Philip Wittenberg; *and
wood engravings by* John De Pol;
compiled and designed by Harvey
Satenstein.

Published by
ACROPOLIS BOOKS LTD.
MCMLXXIII

ACROPOLIS BOOKS LTD.
Colortone Building, 2400 17th St., N.W.
Washington, D. C. 20009

Printed in the United States of America by
COLORTONE PRESS, Creative Graphics Inc.
Washington, D. C. 20009

Library of Congress Catalogue Number 72-12396

Standard Book No. 87491-146-X

PUBLISHER'S NOTE

IT IS A PRIVILEGE to take a leaf out of the notebooks of our Eighteenth Century predecessors and act as both publisher and printer, by publishing this American classic.

Franklin's eloquence about the value of a free press to a free people is especially worth hearing and heeding now. It also points out that attempts to suppress freedom of the press have been with us for a long time.

This edition was first published as a separate volume on the 250th anniversary of Benjamin Franklin's birth to reaffirm the principles for which he stood as printer and statesman. With the approaching Bicentennial of the founding of the Republic, the republication at this time is especially appropriate.

The format and style of this edition is in keeping with the spirit of Franklin to remind us of the great and rich heritage of the dissemination of ideas through the print media.

We are indebted to Harvey Satenstein, the original compiler and designer of this book, for assigning this work to Acropolis Books and Colortone Press to keep this landmark volume in print.

A. J. H.

Books won't stay banned. They won't burn. Ideas won't go to jail. In the long run of history, the censor and the inquisitor have always lost. The only sure weapon against bad ideas is better ideas. The source of better ideas is wisdom. The surest path to wisdom is a liberal education.*

*Alfred Whitney Griswold, *Essays in Education*, Yale University Press.

PREFACE

AT THE AGE OF SIXTEEN Benjamin Franklin had already been seasoned as a printer who had experienced criticism and repression. His brother James had in 1720 or '21 begun to print a newspaper, the *"New England Courant"*, the fifth that had appeared in America.

As Franklin writes in his Autobiography:

"One of the pieces in our newspaper on some political point, which I have now forgotten, gave offense to the Assembly. He was taken up, censur'd and imprison'd for a month, by the speaker's warrant, I suppose, because he would not discover his author. I too was taken up and examin'd before the council; but, tho' I did not give them any satisfaction, they content'd

ix

themselves with admonishing me, and
dismissed me, considering me, perhaps,
as an apprentice, who was bound to
keep his master's secrets.

During my brother's confinement,
which I resented a good deal, notwithstanding our private differences, I had
the management of the paper; and I
made bold to give our rulers some
rubs in it, which my brother took very
kindly, while others began to consider
me in an unfavorable light, as a young
genius that had a turn for libelling
and satire. My brother's discharge was
accompany'd with an order of the
House (a very odd one), that 'James
Franklin should no longer print the
paper called the New England Courant.'"

His brother evaded the order by return-
ing to Benjamin his indenture of apprenticeship thus making it possible for the
paper to be printed under the name of
Benjamin Franklin.

Franklin's experience was not novel, for
up to that time the history of printing had
run parallel with a story of suppression.
Johann Gutenberg's invention of movable

type in 1440 was followed shortly by the establishment in England of the first press by William Caxton. He had learned the art on the Continent and coming to Westminster had set up a press at "The Red Pail" in Almanary. A hundred years after the invention of the movable type we have the first repressive statute passed in 1553 under Henry VIII and by 1556 the Stationers Company was chartered by Philip and Mary.

One of the obvious purposes of the chartering of the Stationers Company was to prevent the diffusion of literature attacking the Church and State, for the Charter itself stated that seditious and heretical books, both in rhymes and tracts, "were daily printed, renewing and spreading detestable heresies against the Catholic doctrine of the Holy Mother Church." The Charter provided for the suppression of the evil by constituting some ninety-seven persons as an incorporated society of the art of stationer, and ordered that no person not a member could practice the

art of printing. Years later our Supreme
Court was to say of the Stationers Company "they were particularly ruthless and
exercised the power of search, confiscation
and imprisonment without interruption
from Parliament."

As usual, however, men of wit and learn-
ing found ways of circumventing statutes
and organizations designed to limit or
prohibit a free press. Secret presses sprang
up. In fact the Star Chamber Decree in
1637 refers to "a great part of the secret
printing in corners" and made provision
for all printing in corners without li-
cense. . . . Like all prohibitory laws evasion
brought about frequent reaffirmation. So
we find orders of the Star Chamber in
1556, 1585, 1623 and 1637.

On the 11th of July, 1637 the Star
Chamber issued its most famous decree.
It ordered:

> "That no person or persons what-
> soeuer shall presume to print, or cause
> to be printed, either in the parts beyond
> the Seas, or in this Realme, or other
> his Maiesties Dominions, any seditious,

scismaticall or offensive Bookes or
Pamphlets, to the scandall of Religion, or the Church, or the Government, or Governours of the Church
or State, or Commonwealth, or of any
Corporation, or particular person or
persons whatsoeuer."

Among its provisions was one that all
books were to have imprinted thereon the
name and address of the publisher and
of the author. The purpose was for identi-
fication for punishment.

When the Star Chamber was abolished
in 1640 by act of Parliament the House
of Commons set up a licensing scheme to
suppress the critical press, and in March
of 1642 they enacted a law providing for a
Committee for Examinations which had
power to search "for presses that are kept
and employed in the printing of scandalous
and lying pamphlets", and in June of 1643
Parliament issued its famous order on the
subject where again they confessed that
their previous orders had failed notwithstanding the diligence of the Company
of Stationers. Its preamble provided:

> "Whereas divers good Orders have
> bin lately made by both Houses of
> Parliament, for suppressing the great
> late abuses and frequent disorders
> in Printing many, false forged, scan-
> dalous, seditious, libellous, and un-
> licensed Papers, Pamphlets, and Books
> to the great defamation of Religion
> and government."

It was this Statute which indirectly was
responsible for the writing of the great
"Areopagitica", John Milton's tract on
unlicensed printing, which appeared on
November 24th, 1634, and which was published unlicensed and unregistered.

After the restoration of the Stuarts came
the Act of King Charles II, which provide
in part:

> "Whereas the well government and
> regulating of printers and printing
> presses is matter of public care and of
> great concernment, especially consider-
> ing, that, by the general licentiousness
> of the late times, many evil-disposed
> persons have been encouraged to print
> and sell heretical, schismatical, blas-
> phemous, seditious, and treasonable
> books, pamphlets, and papers, and

xiv

still do continue such their unlawful
and exorbitant practice, to the high
dishonor of Almighty God, the endan-
gering the peace of these kingdoms,
and raising a disaffection to his most
excellent Majesty and his government;
* * *"

Throughout the existence of these laws
the system of licensing and of the imprimatur was kept alive. The imprimatur
survived as did the decrees as late as 1719
in the province of Massachusetts Bay, and
was in effect during Franklin's early apprenticeship to his brother.

The remembrance of events by the Colo-
nists led to the adoption in the Constitutions of the several states of guarantees
of a free press. The First Amendment to
the Constitution of the United States provided; "Congress shall make no law * * *
abridging freedom of speech or of the
press". Many of the state Constitutions
gave added force to the lesson of history
by the use of the words "printing press"
instead of "press", for the printing press
itself had been deemed the enemy.

The passage of such constitutional clauses and of statutes to enforce and limit them has not brought freedom to the printer. Practically all of our states have laws limiting the press under one guise or another, whether such laws be aimed at what is called obscenity, libel or otherwise. In fact, although Massachusetts had passed its Constitution in 1780 establishing a free press, the record shows at least three convictions for libelous political attacks obtained between 1799 and 1803. The Constitution of Massachusetts, Declaration of Rights, Article 17 provides:

"The liberty of the press is essential to the security of freedom in a state; it ought not, therefore, to be restrained in this commonwealth."

Franklin and the other printers of the colonies had not fought in vain. Every prosecution of a printer brought forth protest. The Constitutions of the several states prove how effective that protest was. From the invention of movable type till today every age has had men like Franklin who keep alive the consciences of men and

the right to the free diffusion of knowledge and opinion.

Constitutional provisions are not enough. Without the eternal struggle for law the press will be enchained. Today, like yesterday, law must be fought for. The printer who would have the courage to print what must be printed must be prepared to meet and struggle with the forces of suppression.

PHILIP WITTENBERG

*Lecturer in Law in
Columbia University*

INTRODUCTION

B. FRANKLIN, PRINTER are the words engraved on the tombstone in the little cemetery, adjoining Christ Church in Philadelphia to mark the grave of a man whose many-sided genius entitled him to much finer-sounding and more important epithets. But he composed this epitaph himself, in a fit of strange humor, when he went into business on his own in 1728, and thought it only natural that he should be remembered as a printer, since his devotion to the trade had begun in early youth and would persist undiminished to the end of his life.

As a boy of twelve, Ben was apprenticed to his brother, James, who was a master printer, and went to work in the latter's

shop in Boston. His diligence, ingenuity, and skill soon enabled him to progress fast enough to direct the affairs of the paper before his term of indenture had expired. But constant quarrels with his brother caused him to break his apprenticeship and run away to New York. That city had no work to offer the ambitious youth at the time, so he continued on to Philadelphia, where he found a job as a journeyman in the printing shop of Samuel Keimer. He was then only nineteen. About a year later, still restless and adventurous, Franklin was on his way to London. In the English capital he worked at his trade in the printing establishments of Palmer and Watts, two of the largest and best equipped in the country, where he learned the most advanced techniques then in use. By the end of 1726 Franklin was back in Philadelphia, again in the employ of Keimer, but his mind was now occupied with plans for starting his own business. With the financial aid of a partner, Franklin ordered a press and types from London, and when the new equipment arrived early in 1728, he was ready to strike out on his own.

From Keimer, his former boss, who was
now in financial difficulties, Franklin
bought a weekly newspaper that bore the
pretentious title of *The Universal Instructor
in All Arts and Sciences and Pennsylvania
Gazette*. The new owner refurbished the
paper, making it lively and topical, re-
christened it simply *The Pennsylvania Gazette*,
and brought out his first issue on October
2, 1729. The paper prospered and led to
further lucrative activities, such as the
yearly publication of the *Poor Richard Al-
manac*, to job and book printing, and to the
printing of public documents and paper
money for the various colonial govern-
ments. In 1748, after twenty years of labor
at his trade, Franklin virtually retired from
active business to devote himself to public
affairs and scientific experiments; but he
had established partnerships with at least
a dozen men, whom he had set up in the
trade in various parts of the country, sup-
plying them with capital and equipment,
in return for a share in their profits. These
partnerships, as Carl Van Doren points
out, were entered into "almost as much to

encourage printing and printers as to bring a return on his money."

The quality of the printing Franklin did during the period when he was establishing his reputation and founding his fortune was remarkable for little more than its neatness and readability; but in his later years in England and France, he continued to run a press and came more and more to be interested in printing as an art. At the age of 74, he was operating his own private press in France with the aid of a foreman and three or four assistants. There he cast type in his own foundry and composed and printed off his essays with his own hands. We are therefore not surprised at the order of the opening words of his last will and testament: "I, Benjamin Franklin, Printer, late Minister Plenipotentiary from the United States of America to the Court of France, now President of Pennsylvania . . ." for these words make it abundantly clear that to this man his life-long trade was of greater significance than the highest honors that his nation and state could bestow upon him.

Since printer's ink never ceased to flow in Franklin's veins, is it any wonder that from his pen should have come a most cogent and definitive statement in defense of freedom of the press? The feature article in *The Pennsylvania Gazette*, for the week June 3 to June 10, 1731, was entitled *An Apology for Printers*. It was Franklin's reply to certain members of the citizenry who were outraged by a statement made in an advertisement which issued from his press. Franklin had printed a handbill from copy submitted to him by the captain of a sailing vessel who was seeking additional freight and passengers; a line at the bottom of the "ad" asked prospective applicants to Note Well (N.B.—Nota Bene): "No Sea-hens nor Black Gowns will be admitted on any terms." People took offense at the words "Sea-hens" and "Black Gowns".

In defending himself, Franklin stated that he knew that the expression "Black Gowns" referred to the clergy of the Church of England, but did not think that the members of the clergy, many of whom were his personal friends, would be dis-

turbed by its use; as for the expression
"Sea-hens," he claimed he had never heard
of it. Here, it appears, he was merely
being discreet, for it seems highly unlikely
that Franklin, who was a master of the
language, had no notion of the meaning
of the word "Sea-hen" since the diction-
aries of the period define "hen" as slang
for whore. Further doubt is thrown upon
his protestations of ignorance when we
examine one of the letters that he wrote,
under the pseudonym of Silence Dogood,
for his brother James' newspaper, *The
New-England Courant*. Ben was only sixteen
years old at the time, but he records his
observations of the behavior of some sailors
and their girls in highly sophisticated sea-
slang. He wrote: "In one of the late pleas-
ant moonlight evenings, I so far indulged
in myself the humor of the town in walk-
ing abroad as to continue from my lodg-
ings two or three hours later than usual. . . .
I met a crowd of Tarpaulins and their
doxies, linked to each other by the arms,
who ran (by their own account) after the
rate of *six knots an hour*, and bent their course

toward the Common. Their eager and amorous emotions of body, occasioned by taking their mistresses *in tow*, they called *wild steerage;* and as a pair of them happened to trip and come to the ground, the company were called upon to *bring to*, for that Jack and Betty were *foundered*. But this fleet were not less comical than a company of females I soon after came up with, who, by throwing their heads to the right and left at everyone who passed by them, I concluded came out with no other design than to revive the spirit of love in disappointed bachelors, and expose themselves to sale to the first bidder. . . ."

Whether Franklin was actually innocently unaware of the meaning of the words he had printed in the advertisement, or only pretended to be so, is, of course, immaterial. Franklin's reaction to the attack which followed was an exact parallel to that of John Milton, who wrote a series of anonymous pamphlets favoring divorce, when his own marriage went sour, and then while the authorities were out looking for the culprit who had dared to pub-

lish such sacrilegious material, composed in self-defense his brilliant *Areopagitica*, the most celebrated plea in English for freedom of the press. So while speaking in his own behalf, Franklin was serving as the mouthpiece for the printing brotherhood of all times.

In view of the fact that Benjamin Franklin has always been known as "The Patron Saint of Printers" and has been quoted as such in season and out, it seems strange that *An Apology for Printers*, his most outspoken statement in support of the members of the trade, has never before been separately printed. It is offered here for the first time to commemorate the 225th anniversary of its original appearance. The spelling, capitalization, and punctuation have been modernized in the present text, since it is more important for us to preserve the timeliness and clarity of Franklin's ideas than his eighteenth-century manuscript style. Thanks are due to Mr. Archibald Hanna, Librarian in charge of the Benjamin Franklin Collection, Yale University Library for supply-

ing me with a photostatic copy of the original article.

This little keepsake is intended to show, as if additional proof were needed, on the eve of the 250th anniversary of his birth, that to Benjamin Franklin the smell of printer's ink was as frankincense and myrrh, and that by his solemn devotion to the printed word he was able to leave the imprint of his unique mind and spirit upon the world.

RANDOLPH GOODMAN

Brooklyn College

An Apology for Printers

An Apology for Printers

BEING FREQUENTLY CENSURED and condemned by different persons for printing things which they say ought not to be printed, I have sometimes thought it might be necessary to make a standing apology for myself, and publish it once a year, to be read upon all occasions of that nature. Much business has hitherto hindered the execution of this design; but having very lately given extraordinary offence by printing an advertisement with a certain N.B. at the end of it, I find an apology more particularly requisite at this juncture, though it happens when I have not yet leisure to write such a thing in the proper

form, and can only in a loose manner throw those considerations together which should have been the substance of it.

I request all who are angry with me on the account of printing things they don't like, calmly to consider these following particulars:

1. That the opinions of men are almost as various as their faces; an observation general enough to become a common proverb, *So many men so many minds;*

2. That the business of printing has chiefly to do with men's opinions; most things that are printed tending to promote some, or oppose others;

3. That hence arises the peculiar unhappiness of that business, which other callings are no way liable to; they who follow printing being scarce able to do anything in their way of getting a living, which shall not probably give offence to some, and perhaps to many; whereas the smith, the shoemaker, the carpenter, or the man of any other trade,

4

may work indifferently for people of all persuasions, without offending any of them; and the merchant may buy and sell with Jews, Turks, heretics and infidels of all sorts, and get money by every one of them, without giving offence to the most orthodox, of any sort; or suffering the least censure or ill-will on the account from any man whatever;

4. That it is as unreasonable in any one man or set of men to expect to be pleased with everything that is printed, as to think that nobody ought to be pleased but themselves;

5. Printers are educated in the belief, that when men differ in opinion, both sides ought equally to have the advantage of being heard by the public; and that when truth and error have fair play, the former is always an overmatch for the latter. Hence they cheerfully serve all contending writers that pay them well, without regarding on

which side they are of the question in dispute;

6. Being thus continually employed in serving both parties, printers naturally acquire a vast unconcernedness as to the right or wrong opinions contained in what they print; regarding it only as the matter of their daily labor. They print things full of spleen and animosity, with the utmost calmness and indifference, and without the least ill-will to the persons reflected on, who nevertheless unjustly think the printer as much their enemy as the author, and join both together in their resentment;

7. That it is unreasonable to imagine printers approve of everything they print, and to censure them on any particular thing accordingly; since in the way of their business they print such great variety of things opposite and contradictory. It is likewise as unreasonable what some assert, "That printers

ought not to print anything but what they approve;" since if all of that business should make such a resolution, and abide by it, an end would thereby be put to free writing, and the world would afterwards have nothing to read but what happened to be the opinions of printers;

8. That if all printers were determined not to print anything till they were sure it would offend nobody, there would be very little printed;

9. That if they sometimes print vicious or silly things not worth reading, it may not be because they approve such things themselves, but because the people are so viciously and corruptly educated that good things are not encouraged. I have known a very numerous impression of Robin Hood's songs go off in this province at 2 s. per book, in less than a twelvemonth; when a small quantity of David's Psalms (an

7

excellent version) has lain upon my hands above twice the time;

10. That notwithstanding what might be urged in behalf of a man's being allowed to do in the way of his business whatever he is paid for, yet printers do continually discourage the printing of great numbers of bad things, and stifle them in the birth. I myself have constantly refused to print anything that might countenance vice, or promote immorality; though by complying in such cases with the corrupt taste of the majority I might have got much money. I have also always refused to print such things as might do real injury to any person, how much soever I have been solicited, and tempted with offers of great pay; and how much soever I have by refusing got the ill-will of those who would have employed me. I have hitherto fallen under the resentment of large bodies of men, for refusing abso-

lutely to print any of their party or personal reflections. In this manner I have made myself many enemies, and the constant fatigue of denying is almost insupportable. But the public being unacquainted with all this, whenever the poor printer happens either through ignorance or much persuasion, to do anything that is generally thought worthy of blame, he meets with no more friendship or favor on the above account, than if there were no merit in it at all. Thus, as Waller says,

> *Poets lose half the praise they would have got*
> *Were it but known what they discreetly blot;*

yet are censured for every bad line found in their works with the utmost severity.

I come now to the particular case of the N. B. above-mentioned, about which there has been more clamor against me,

than ever before on any other account.

In the hurry of other business an advertisement was brought to me to be printed. It signified that such a ship lying at such a wharf would sail for Barbados in such a time, and that freighters and passengers might agree with the captain at such a place. So far is what's common; but at the bottom this odd thing was added, "N. B. No Sea-hens nor Black Gowns will be admitted on any terms." I printed it, and received my money; and the advertisement was stuck up round the town as usual. I had not so much curiosity at that time as to enquire the meaning of it, nor did I in the least imagine it would give so much offence. Several good men are very angry with me on this occasion. They are pleased to say I have too much sense to do such things ignorantly, that if they were printers they would not have done such a thing on any consideration, that it could proceed from nothing but my abundant malice against religion and the clergy. They therefore declare they will not take any more of my papers, nor have any further

dealings with me, but will hinder me of all the custom they can. All this is very hard!

I believe it had been better if I had refused to print the said advertisement. However, it's done, and cannot be revoked. I have only the following few particulars to offer, some of them in my behalf, by way of mitigation, and some not much to the purpose; but I desire none of them may be read when the reader is not in a very good humor:

1. That I really did it without the least malice, and imagined the N. B. was placed there only to make the advertisement stared at, and more generally read;

2. That I never saw the word Sea-hens before in my life; nor have I yet asked the meaning of it. And though I had certainly known that Black Gowns in that place signi-fied the clergy of the Church of England, yet I have that confidence in the generous good temper of such of them as I know, as to be well satisfied such a trifling mention

11

of their habit gives them no disturbance;

3. That most of the clergy in this and the neighboring provinces, are my customers, and some of them my very good friends; and I must be very malicious, indeed, or very stupid, to print this thing for a small profit, if I had thought it would have given them just cause of offence;

4. That if I had much malice against the clergy, and withal much sense, it's strange I never write or talk against the clergy myself. Some have observed that it's a fruitful topic, and the easiest to be witty upon of all others; yet I appeal to the public that I am never guilty this way, and to all my acquaintances as to my conversation;

5. That if a man of sense had malice enough to desire to injure the clergy, this is the most foolish thing he could possibly contrive for that purpose;

12

6. That I got five shillings by it;
7. That none who are angry with me would have given me so much to let it alone;
8. That if all the people of different opinions in this province would engage to give me as much for not printing things they don't like, as I can get by printing them, I should probably live a very easy life; and if all printers were everywhere so dealt by, there would be very little printed;
9. That I am obliged to all who take my paper, and am willing to think they do it out of mere friendship. I only desire they would think the same when I deal with them. I thank those who leave off, that they have taken it so long. But I beg they would not endeavor to dissuade others, for that will look like malice;
10. That it's impossible any man should know what he would do if he were a printer;

13

11. That notwithstanding the rashness and inexperience of youth, which is most likely to be prevailed upon to do things that ought not to be done, yet I have avoided printing such things as usually give offence either to church or state, more than any printer that has followed the business in this province before;

12. And lastly, that I have printed above a thousand advertisements which made not the least mention of *Sea-hens* or *Black Gowns;* and this being the first offence, I have the more reason to expect forgiveness.

I take leave to conclude with an old fable, which some of my readers have heard before, and some have not:

"A certain well-meaning man and his son were travelling towards a market town with an ass which they had to sell. The road was bad, and the old man therefore rode, but the son went afoot. The first passerby they met asked the father

14

if he was not ashamed to ride by himself, and suffer the poor lad to wade along through the mire; this induced him to take up his son behind him. He had not travelled far, when he met others, who said, they are two unmerciful lubbers to get both on the back of that poor ass in such a deep road. Upon this the old man got off, and let his son ride alone. The next they met called the lad a graceless, rascally young jackanapes, to ride in that manner through the dirt, while his aged father trudged along on foot; and they said the old man was a fool for suffering it. He then bid his son come down, and walk with him, and they travelled on leading the ass by the halter, till they met another company, who called them a couple of senseless blockheads, for going both on foot in such a dirty way, when they had an empty ass with them, which they might ride upon. The old man

could bear it no longer. 'My son,' said he, 'it grieves me much that we cannot please all these people. Let me throw the ass over the next bridge, and be no further troubled with him.' "

Had the old man been seen acting this last resolution, he would probably have been called a fool for troubling himself about the different opinions of all that were pleased to find fault with him. Therefore, though I have a temper almost as complying as his, I intend not to imitate him in this last particular. I consider the variety of humors among men, and despair of pleasing everybody; yet I shall not therefore leave off printing. I shall continue my business. I shall not burn my press and melt my letters.

16